Hunt the Cupcake!

Hunt the Cupcake!

A bumper collection of fiendishly
difficult Hunt the Cupcake challenges

Siân Keogh

Bet you can't find them all!

FIREFLY BOOKS

A FIREFLY BOOK

Published by Firefly Books Ltd. 2009

First printing

Publisher Cataloging-in-Publication Data (U.S.)

Keogh, Sian, 1967-
Hunt the cupcake : a bumper collection of fiendishly
difficult hunt the cupcake challenges / Sian Keogh.
[144] p. : col. ill., photos. ; cm.
ISBN-13: 978-1-55407-508-9 (pbk.)
ISBN-10: 1-55407-508-4 (pbk.)
1. Picture puzzles. I. Title.

793.73 dc22 GV1507.P47K436 2009

Library and Archives Canada Cataloguing in Publication

Keogh, Sian, 1967-
Hunt the cupcake : a bumper collection of fiendishly difficult hunt the
cupcake challenges / Sian Keogh.
ISBN-13: 978-1-55407-508-9
ISBN-10:1-55407-508-4
1. Picture puzzles. I. Title.

GV1507.P47K464 2009   793.73   C2009-901475-0

Published in the United States by
Firefly Books (U.S.) Inc.
P.O. Box 1338, Ellicott Station
Buffalo, New York 14205

Published in Canada by
Firefly Books Ltd.
66 Leek Crescent
Richmond Hill, Ontario L4B 1H1

Printed in China

Hunt the Cupcake!

How to use this book

The heading will tell you how many cupcakes are hidden in the picture.

Some cupcakes will be easy to spot, while others will be a little more elusive, as only a small part of the cupcake will be visible.

The original puzzle page numbers are clearly labeled under each picture.

The answers:

HUNT THE CUPCAKE!

PAGES 106–107

PAGES 110–111

PAGES 108–109

142

PAGES 112–113

143

The centers of the red and yellow circles indicate the position of each cupcake hidden in the picture.

The puzzles

Find 6 cupcakes

Find 8 cupcakes

Find 8 cupcakes

Find 6 cupcakes

Find 7 cupcakes

Find 6 cupcakes

Find 6 cupcakes

Find 6 cupcakes

Find 6 cupcakes

Find 6 cupcakes

Find 6 cupcakes

Find 6 cupcakes

Find 6 cupcakes

Find 6 cupcakes

Find 6 cupcakes

Find 8 cupcakes

Find 6 cupcakes

Find 6 cupcakes

Find 6 cupcakes

Find 5 cupcakes

The answers:

PAGES 10–11

PAGES 12–13

PAGES 14–15

PAGES 16–17

The answers:

PAGES 18–19

PAGES 20–21

PAGES 22–23

PAGES 24–25

The answers:

PAGES 26–27

PAGES 28–29

PAGES 30–31

PAGES 32–33

The answers:

PAGES 34–35

PAGES 36–37

PAGES 38–39

PAGES 40–41

The answers:

PAGES 42–43

PAGES 44–45

PAGES 46–47

PAGES 48–49

The answers:

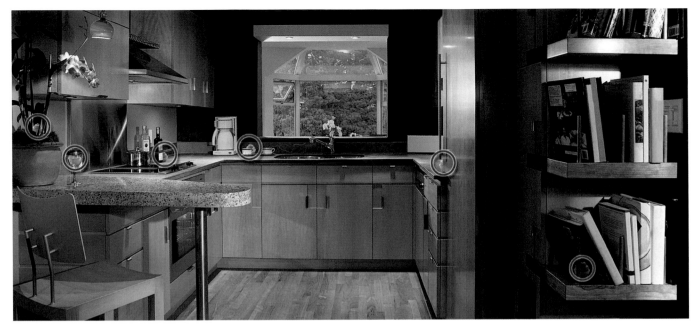

PAGES 50–51

PAGES 52–53

PAGES 54–55

PAGES 56–57

The answers:

PAGES 58–59

PAGES 60–61

PAGES 62–63

PAGES 64–65

The answers:

PAGES 66–67

PAGES 68–69

PAGES 70–71

PAGES 72–73

The answers:

PAGES 74–75

PAGES 76–77

PAGES 78–79

PAGES 80–81

The answers:

PAGES 82–83

PAGES 84–85

PAGES 86–87

PAGES 88–89

The answers:

PAGES 90–91

PAGES 92–93

PAGES 94–95

PAGES 96–97

The answers:

PAGES 98–99

PAGES 100–101

PAGES 102–103

PAGES 104–105

The answers:

PAGES 106–107

PAGES 108–109

PAGES 110–111

PAGES 112–113

The answers:

PAGES 114–115

PAGES 116–117